SENSE OF ACTION (KARMA)

(BASED ON BHAGAVAD GITA CHAPTER-3)

DR. JAGADEESH PILLAI

Copyright © Dr. Jagadeesh Pillai
All Rights Reserved.

"All THOSE WHO ARE IN SEARCH OF CORRECT PATH OF ACTION"

Contents

Prayer   *vii*

About The Author   *ix*

Preface   *xv*

Sense Of Action (Karma)

Chapter-3 Slokhas In English Text For Quick Reference

Contact   53

Prayer

HARE RAMA HARE RAMA, RAMA RAMA HARE HARE
- HARE KRISHNA, HARE KRISHNA, KRISHNA
KRISHNA, HARE HARE

(Mantra - Kali Santaranopanishad)

About The Author

Dr. Jagadeesh Pillai a voracious reader, Four Times Guinness World Record holder, writer, and true research scholar was born in Varanasi, the abode of Lord Shiva. He is Ph.D. in Vedic Science. He is a multi-faceted polymath with innate qualities, creative ideas and many remarkable achievements. Although his roots extend back to "Gods own Country"(Kerala), the residents of Varanasi feel proud of him and adore him as a child of Varanasi who caters to every individual in need without any expectations. A deep study into his profile reflects that he has added so many feathers to his cap which makes him quite unique. He is a four times Guinness Book of World Records Holder in the following subjects :

"Script to Screen" which he achieved by producing and directing a state of art animation film within the shortest time possible by breaking the earlier set record by Canadians. There are many national and international Awards and Recognitions to his credit.

Longest Line of Post Cards which he has done on the occasion of 163 years of Indian Postal Day by 16300 post cards. The event was also connected with a questionnaire about Indian Flag.

Largest Poster Awareness Campaign – This was achieved by designing an awareness campaign on the subject "Beti Bachao – Beti Padhao".

Largest Envelop – Towards tribute to Prime Minister's

initiative 'Make in India' – he has created about 4000 sq meter envelop using waste papers.

Attempted by lighting 70000 candles on a 210 kg cake to celebrate the 70th Indian Independence day recorded in World Records India.

Attempted a documentary on Dhamek Stupa of Sarnath dubbing in 17 languages, result is waiting from Guinness World Records.

He is versatile in Gita teaching. The young generation is fond of his Gita teaching and he has changed the life of many young through his continued motivational boost up and teachings.

He has composed and sung Gayatri Mantra in 1000 different tunes.

He has composed and sung Hanuman Chalisa in 108 different tunes.

He has composed and sung hundreds of Sanskrit Bhajans, Patriotic songs, etc.

He has written and directed so many short films and documentaries for awareness campaigns.

He has done voluntary services to UP Police and Kerala Police to spread awareness campaigns on the various issue through videos and photography.

He is on the path of authoring thousands of books on Indian culture, Indian Temples, and the life of extraordinary people.

It is hard to believe that he has produced and directed more than 100 Documentaries on a particular city (Varanasi) which is done by a single person.

He has helped and guided more than 25 boys and girls to achieve world records through various creative and innovative methods.

A multifaceted person who can apply the best of his intellect using the God-given blessings which have been showered upon every human being granting them an immense capacity to learn, experience, and experiment with many things and do wonders in this world of discrimination and disparities.

He is a teacher and a student at the same time who always learns every day and teaches every day. As a master, his weakness was that he never sticks to a particular subject. Perhaps this weakness gives him the strength to master any area which he came across.

Each of his days dawned with learning a new topic and he spend most of his time experimenting and researching it.

He is also a selfless social activist and a motivational speaker.

His life was full of struggle, ups and downs, and failures. But he never gave up and faced all his trials and tribulations full of confidence. Today he is a successful young man with a lot of enthusiasm and rich life experience.

He has sung full Ram Charita Manas 51 hours audio by his own composition. He has also sung the whole Bhagavad-Gita in his own composition with a rhythmic background.

He has also sung "Lokah Samastha Sukhino Bhavantu" in 50 different languages.

Currently working on a detailed and scientific study on Veda, Upanishad, Puranas, Bhagavad Gita, etc.

Currently, he is the Hon' Chancellor of 'Eurasia Digital University'.

Awards

Four Times Guinness World Records

Winner of Mahatma Gandhi Vishwa Shanti Puraskar

Mahatma Gandhi Global Peace Ambassador

Kashi Ratna Award

Dr. APJ Abdul Kalam Motivational Person of the Year 2017

Mother Teresa Award

Indira Gandhi Priyadarshini Award

Bharat Vikas Ratna Award

Udyog Ratna Award

Vigyan Prasar Award

Poorvanchal Ratn Samman

Preface

KARMA (ACTION) - One of the most important parts of Chapter-3 of Bhagavad Gita and even the most important thing one must understand and must be followed to excel in every part of life doing multiple karmas (actions), without any hesitation or regrets.

Most of the people don't understand the exact meaning of Karma (action). Doing any activity through the hand, legs, and mouth is not Karma.

What is Karma, Dharma etc. has been simply explained in this book by the author with the modern way of understanding especially for the new generation to understand.

Sense of Action (Karma)

KARMA (ACTION) - One of the most important parts of this chapter and even the most important thing one must understand and must be followed to excel in every part of life doing multiple karmas (actions), without any hesitation or regrets.

Most of the people don't understand the exact meaning of Karma (action). Doing any activity through the hand, legs, and mouth is not Karma.

Let's classify it through an example :

Two persons of your nearby locality have opened two separate provisional stores to supply different grains and food items.

We asked the first person, why did you open the store?

"He said, to make money out of it"

We again asked, do you offer discounts and help to poor people?

He said, No...I don't offer any discounts and nothing to do with poor people, I am here for making money, if you pay, I will sell, that's all. The more I earn, I am happy.

Then we asked the 2nd person, why did you open the store?

"He said, to serve the people of my locality"

Do you offer discounts and help to poor people?

He said, Yes…I do offer discounts to everybody wherever possible and will be giving more discounts to poor people, I am here to serve people, not just to earn, I will still earn whatever needed from the margin I get and I am happy.

See, what is the difference here…

Both are doing some action (karma) by selling the same thing, both will earn money. But only the intention of both is different.

1. Selfish Action

2. Selfless Action

Selfish Action is called – KRIYA

Selfless Action is called – KARMA

Whatever action we do for ourselves, with a selfish mentality like "for money, for me and my family only" – is called KRIYA.

Suppose if one person is working for a company for 8 hours daily, from 9 AM to 5 PM for a salary of Rs. 50,000 per month and just after 5 PM every day, he leaves the company, back home and spends time with his family.

If we ask him what action he did today?, he will reply, "I went for my job, performed my 8 hours of duty, and returned home". His understanding of action (karma) goes this way. He understands that his official duty is actually the action (karma).

If the boss of the company by chance requests him to do one more hour after 5 PM for few days in a month, he will say that he needs to pay overtime for that unless he won't do.

So whatever he does for office is connected with selfish intention.

Whatever he considers as action (karma) is not exactly karma, but is called "KRIYA". He is doing the job for his salary for the existence of his and to feed his family. His life is limited to earning and feeding his own family. Here he does everything to satisfy himself but does nothing to satisfy his Soul/Supreme.

If he happily accepted the proposal when the boss requested him to do the extra one-hour duty without expecting any remuneration, it is considered as "selfless action - karma" in other words "sacrifice".

Selfless Action – Karma - sacrifices - gives satisfaction.

Selfish Karma – Kriya - me-mine attitude - develops selfishness

<u>Origin of the term "Sanatana Dharma"</u>

If we ask anybody especially in India, what is Sanatana Dharma, they will immediately say "Hindu Religion". This is a wrong comment.

Even if ask what is "Dharma" – again many people answer it as "Religion". Again a wrong answer.

Let' decode it here.

"Sanatana" –

means - permanent, for a long time, since long time..etc.

"Dharma" –

Means - a selfless action done as an obligatory duty.

Let's go through an example :

We all are taking oxygen from nature for our breathing. Breathing is un-avoidable. In hospitals when in an emergency if we need an oxygen cylinder, we need to pay approx. Rs. 700 per day.

But we get free oxygen from nature. If we have to pay daily Rs. 700 x 30 days = 21000 x 12 months = Rs. 2,52,000 per year.

Suppose we live for approx. 80 years, 80 x Rs. 2,52,000 = Approx. Rs. 2 Crore oxygen we needed for 80 years of breathing and survival.

From where we get this oxygen? - From plants and trees.

Did you ever plant and cultivated all those plants and trees which give you oxygen? No.

Somebody else planted. We are just using it free of cost.

So, when you understood this reality about the oxygen which you are consuming daily for your survival, you can still develop two thoughts within you depending on the purity of your mind.

Selfish thoughts – I do not want to bother who has planted, just consume and enjoy life. I am not even bothered to think about the future generation.

Selfless thoughts – Since I am taking oxygen from the plants, which are cultivated by others, then it is my duty and obligation to cultivate more plants towards reciprocation and for the future generation to come. Future generation includes our grandchildren, great-grandchildren and so on.

When this selfless thought emerged in your mind, the next day, you brought some seeds, cultivated it in your land or nearby, and started looking after to it by giving water, fertilizer, etc. *(without publicity, if it was done for publicity, the action will be treated as selfish action – done for name & fame).*

A few years later, out of the many plants you have cultivated, one plant came up well and became a big tree.

Now, few questions...

Will this plant die, the day you die? **No**...it will remain there for **so long (unlimited times – Sanatan times").**

Can you count how much oxygen is generated from this tree? **No.** *Cores and crores, un-measurable.*

Can you exactly find out how many persons benefited from it? **No.** *Unlimited people, unlimited way, un-measurable.*

Can you check, how many more trees might have grown up by the seeds of the same tree which you have planted? **No –** *thousands of more trees might have grown-up by the seeds of this tree.*

Can you check what benefit the other specious like birds etc. availed from the tree? *No. idea....limitless, un-measurable.*

Just imagine that you did a small action (karma) of planting a tree with the selfless thought of benefit to others.

The karma (action) you did as your duty and obligation, the word "karma" has been changed to "dharma". Karma means – action, Dharma means – duty.

An action (Karma) done towards an obligatory duty is called **"DHARMA"**

From the above example,

The tree planted by you is now a big tree and the tree is not going to die, the day you will die. It will be there for unlimited times or permanent. If by chance later sometime the tree dies after you die, there will be many more available which are grownup from the seeds of the tree you have planted.

So the effect of your karma is not going to end even after 1000s of years whether you exist in this world or not.

Doing such Karma (selfless action) as an obligatory duty which remains its permanent effect in the universe even after we die, is called "SANATANA DHARMA".

Nowhere in any book of ancient Indian literature which I referred from Vedas to Purana, nowhere I found the connection of "SANATANA DHARMA" with religious concept.

The teachings you will get from any "Sanatana Dharma" literature is how to do and follow many of such selfless actions (duties and obligations) to have a permanent effect in the universe for the benefit of us and for the benefit of other generations to come.

The most important reason for our creation and our existence on the earth is to do so many selfless karmas as explained earlier for the universe.

Finding food, shelter, earning money, etc. are all part of the requirement for our physical existence, yes it is very much necessary. But ultimately, we are also forced to perform selfless actions like Sun lights the world and purifies everything, every day it performs its selfless duty assigned to it. Sun never expects anything back from anything or anybody. The creator has embedded some quality within it and per that quality, it has to light, distribute energy and purify the nature.

After this explanation, it will be easy to exactly understand the meaning of "Karma" – action. When you act upon with the power and quality embedded within you to light others and light the world towards obligatory duty (swadharma) to the creator, the Supreme i.e. here referred to as "Krishna".

So, in Bhagavad Gita or this book, wherever the word Karma, action, sacrifices, etc. comes, it must be considered as doing selfless karma. Without sacrifice, selfless karma is not possible, that's why both are interconnected.

***

A life story to understand :

There was a professor with a wife and two children. He already belongs to a wealthy family. He has worked in many government colleges and holds a post as Principal.

His wife is also working and holds a high-rank officer post in a government department. Financially well settled. They have one daughter and one son. Daughter is married and she is also a professor in a government college with more than six-figure salary. Their son is still pursuing his post-graduation.

The situation I want to explain is – the parents have already been having their parental wealth, plus they also accumulated through their job and added more wealth and properties from their high salaries. The parents don't get a chance to use their parental wealth because they were already earning more than enough for their daily living and rest they were saving. Their son is still in his post-graduation and expects to be settled very soon.

When their daughter and son will also earn their own enough for their daily living, they are also not going to utilise and consume the wealth and properties of their parents and grandparents.

But the ignorance of Karma (action) starts now.

The father who was a professor and a college principal has retired on completing his 60 years of age. Since he was an excellent teacher of many subjects, he will be getting a handsome pension for his daily living and expenses.

The next week itself, after retirement, he started searching for a new job. No issue, good that he wants to engage in some activity.

Many small and big private colleges have approached him to teach in their colleges. But the problem is his demanding a high salary for his job and finally, he joins a private college as a professor for a high salary again.

The whole life he lived for him and his family and collected enough money and wealth. Never did any notable selfless service for the society. A little bit, as usual, he might have done, but the ratio compared to their wealth and earnings was equal to nothing. The whole life he was busy with his profession, looking after his kids, savings, accumulating properties, etc.

Now even after retirement, he is again teaching for the money.

If he had the "wisdom and understanding" to do some actual karmas (Sanatan Karmas – obligatory actions and duties which have permanent stability with unlimited returns generation by generation), at least after retirement, he has to join a small college and has to offer free teaching for the rest of his life. Or he has to open a coaching center offering free education to financially poor students.

He or his children is not going to enjoy or use the whole wealth and properties he occupied yet. Because a simple health issue or any unforeseen circumstances happens in the future either to him or his children or anyone in his next generation can spoil the whole wealth and properties within no time.

***

Quote to note :

The value of wealth which we have earned through our hard work remains till we live on this earth. For our descendants, it's a free bread, hence no value.

***

But if the teacher at least spends a little bit of time after retirement and teaches a few students who were on the verge to stop their further education because of financial problems, their career improvement and changes in life will be counted as his actual earning through selfless karma that nature counts for him and will remain here permanently. The fruit of it will be enjoyed by many of his own generation and others too for an unlimited time.

Quote to note :

Our future life, the life of next birth, the life of our next-generation is not based on the valueless physical and material wealth we possess but based on the value of selfless actions (karmas) we did.

In some wealthy families (accumulated through generations), we can see that some children are on the wrong pathway of life with the ego of high wealth and prosperity possesses by their parents. They lavishly enjoy, become drug addicts and spends a lot of money on unnecessary things. Since it was not hard-earned by them, they have no pain to spend it on.

We all can see many such families in our surroundings.

I have very recently witnessed collapsing of a big hospital in my city which has been running for more than a hundred years. Immense wealth was occupied by them. The husband was a builder and his wife was a famous doctor. Their only son and daughter were school toppers. Just within five years all of sudden everything has been collapsed. Builder husband was killed, the school topper son who was pursuing his graduation became a drug addict and was demanding heavy amounts from his mother for the drug. The mother (doctor) went into depression. Son has taken his sister with him so that through her, he can demand money from his mother and her further education was also disturbed. Later the mother has also committed suicide. The hospital and the construction business has been stopped. The drug-addicted son has sold the whole property and shifted to another city with his sister.

If wealth, money and property was everything or important to lie upon why it happened all of sudden.

Quote to note :

Goodness generated through selfless actions (karmas) has its value and sustains to enjoy for the future and to enjoy the next generation to come.

It sustains like Dr. APJ Abdul Kalam's life, attitude, achievements, and teachings, it sustains like the life and teaching of Swami Vivekananda, it sustains like the life, sacrifices, and teachings of Mahatma Gandhi, it sustains like Banaras Hindu University, the capital of knowledge established by Pandit Madan Mohan Malviya.

Quote to note :

Even a new baby who is expected to deliver tomorrow is going to learn from the selfless actions of great people because their goodness will sustain here for an unlimited time.

It was surprised me when a doctor recently rejected my plea to join us to sanitize the people in the vegetable market during the lockdown period. The doctor is not interested to do any selfless service outside his hospital cabin. We should not angry with him for his behavior because of his ignorance and not knowing the importance of selfless karmas.

***

In the 2nd chapter, Krishna has explained the qualities of a self-realized person, explained the importance of controlling the mind and senses and the importance of balancing it. But, no-where given the explanation in detail and about doing actions (karma). If we have the knowledge of balancing the mind and also know to control its senses from desires, why we should give importance to action (karma) (3/1-2).

There are two ways to reach a higher level of spiritual development. _One by achieving wisdom through actions_ and then _by doing actions through wisdom to achieve liberation_.

__*Spiritual development means*__, cutting the ignorance from the mind by cutting the ego, selfishness, me-mine attitude, etc. and developing a balanced mind with compassion, goodness, selfless actions, obligatory duties, forgiveness, gratefulness, etc.

__*Wisdom achievement means,*__ we understand that the authority of every creature on the earth including us is of God and we have to do actions (karmas) for our well being/ self-existence and with that well being and self-existence, we need to serve God (through selfless actions) to satisfy the Soul and the Supreme. If we are not doing the selfless actions, our self-existence and well-being will disbalance.)

Quote to note :

Spiritually developed people with the achievement of the importance of wisdom (knowledge) of selfless actions are called self-realized persons.

It may be a little bit confusing. Let me logically clear it by explaining the driving of a car.

1. Learning driving - action

2. Learned driving – achieved wisdom (knowledge) of driving

3. Doing the job of driving for money, looking after his family and children and for self-existence – *wisdom (knowledge) of driving as action used for it, the action of selfish nature to fulfill his needs and desires to satisfy himself.*

4. By doing the above for money to fulfill his family desires, he also drives an ambulance in the evening for two hours free (selfless karma). He does *selfless action to satisfy the Soul and Supreme by using <u>the wisdom (knowledge) of driving</u> and by understanding the <u>wisdom (knowledge) of the importance of selfless karma</u>.*

(here he earns money through driving job for the family plus by driving the ambulance for free he earns permanent sustainable fruit of karma for mental peace, satisfaction and spiritual development.) One action for himself (fruit of it sustains temporary) – 2nd action for Soul & Supreme (fruit of it unimaginable & unmeasurable but sustains permanent).

One is by achieving knowledge, intelligence and wisdom and another are through action (doing karmas).

The self-realized person who has achieved mental balancing, wisdom, and intelligence, the importance of selfless actions by understanding the Soul and Supreme connectivity, achieves liberation.

(liberation means developing and achieving the higher quality state of spiritual development to reach the Supreme as explained in the previous chapter)

Krishna's disciple, Arjuna has not achieved this level, that's why he was disappointed and surrendered to Krishna to guide on the battlefield. For us, the battlefield is our life. All those who have not yet achieved the above level have still to do a lot of actions through which we can disconnect from desires, bondage, and attachments from physical things and practice to control the mind from desires.

(still, the word "action" may be confusing…what does it actually mean. One must clear it exactly otherwise the whole purpose of our living, the teachings of Gita and even this book is no use for anybody. I will try my best to logically clear it by the end of this chapter.)

***

People want to choose two different pathways to reach the destination per their knowledge, awareness, and understanding that's why Krishna also explains two different ways to reach the same destination, i.e. to attain liberation.

For example, one person is on his travel to reach a destination by car, he almost travelled the most, so he has been suggested a wide road to reach the destination soon. Another person is traveling by bike and still so far to reach and that's why we suggested him a short cut narrow way to reach the destination. The bike can even move through many narrow ways, but the car needed wide roads. The destination is the same.

(1) The person in Car is a highly spiritually developed person with a balanced mind and near to his destination.

(2) The person in the bike is an underdeveloped stage towards attaining higher spiritual intelligence and he has to travel a lot and has to cross many good and bad roads to reach the destination.

Arjuna's mental state was not stable and at the same time, he surrendered himself by withdrawing from his duties and actions saying that he does not want to fight on the battlefield. (for us, our life is the battlefield).

Physical and mental attachment, fear of loss, unaware of the karmic consequences, etc. are confused him, that's why Krishna has explained in the previous chapter not to confuse about the result, just perform your duties for which you are *born, educated and trained*. (3/3)

***

By withdrawing from our duties for what we are born, educated and trained for, we won't attain anything.

Refusing to perform any action either by word, mind or body is not a perfect decision to attain spiritual development and even such people don't achieve anything in life.

A living person cannot sit idle, without doing any action, because the three qualities (gunas) (Chap.14) within you will motivate or force you to perform some duties and action even if you intend to do it or not. Breathing is an example of an action (karma), which we perform regularly without any fail. Shall we withdraw it? No way. So we are forced to perform our duties for which we are born. (3/4-5).

*****

Until now we discuss actions like doing a job, walking, singing, selling, beating, smelling, etc.

But to understand actions (Karma) more in detail we need to study actions (karma) through mind and senses.

Senses can be classified in two ways :

One is actions by organs, and the other is actions by senses.

Senses of action – Vision, Hearing, Touch, Smell, and Taste.

Organs of action – Eyes, Ears, Skin, Nose & Tongue.

We can control our organs of action by controlling our Hands, legs, etc. **but we can't control actions by senses within the mind.**

For example, if we are angry and want to beat somebody but the person is not in our city so we are abusing him, beating him in our mind. *This is a false appearance of virtue.*

We can control the organs by force, but our mind does the action by thoughts, is said to be a hypocrite. So it is necessary to understand the secret of various types of action.

For Example :

Some people do a lot of God worshipping, following fasting, etc. but just after that, they will either by mind or words or in anger will abuse or condemn somebody. Worshipping, fasting, reading spiritual books, etc., are the different ways of cleaning of mind and senses to achieve higher spiritual development. During the period of God worshipping, fasting, etc., the cleaning process of mind happens and some parts of it clean. But when they again immediately involved in the activity of abuse, anger, etc., the mind will dirt again, just like your body was cleaned after bath and just after bath you fell on the mud of outside ground and again the body get dirtied.

A balanced mind and realization of understanding and wisdom are necessary to permanently clean the mind, then only we can reach to a high level of spiritual development. Otherwise, the process of dirt and clean, dirt and clean will continue. No development will happen in life. That's why people do not get any result even doing continued worshipping. They will complain that God is not listening to our prayer. They will not stop reacting to situations by balancing their mind and will continue to abuse and condemn other people or will show jealous of other's growth etc., and by doing it, they will expect blessings and result for their worshipping. (3/6).

Whoever has full control over mind, senses, and desires, unattached to anything, doing selfless karmas without expecting anything in return, even name or fame; such moral people, are the truly dedicated seeker has connection with God. Whatever they do is not to please any person, not to please self, not to win any material thing, rather please the Soul to get a higher level of spiritual development to achieve union with the Supreme. Withdrawing the mind from the physical senses while doing any action will be considered as a true God-uniting activity. (3/7).

For doing whatever karma (action), you are qualified for, you must follow it. Performing your duties of action is much greater than sitting idle. No doubt, for your living, for your family, for food, shelter and for accumulating material wealth, etc., you will be doing some work, job, business, etc. But here, in this chapter, the necessity of doing selfless Karma has emphasized.

Just refer to the 2nd shopkeeper in the above story, who does his business as service not just for earning money. He will get money and he will also be able to fulfill the needs of his family. But still, his intention is not limited to money-making. Here he sacrifices the dirty desire of "money-making only" from his mind, whereas he has been cultivated the pure intention to serve.

Since he has sacrificed the desire while doing the action as a shop keeper, he is not attached or developed any bondage with anything or anybody. He is free from tensions and people around him will also be very happy with his selfless and down-to-earth attitude.

Quote to Note:

More people are happy means, more souls are happy, more souls are happy means, the Supreme is happy.

But what about the 1st Shopkeeper, who opened the same shop with the intention of money-making only, no discounts, no help to anybody. Come, buy, pay and go.

He is addicted and attached to the desire for money-making, connected with his family and relations and always thinking of their well-wishing only because of his selfish mentality with a narrow mind. Most of the boxes of his mind are badly rusted and difficult to open and light up.

The only way to attain everything in life with happiness and permanent peace is to perform <u>selfless actions with sacrifices.</u>

The result and fruit of selfless action are unlimited, un-imaginable, un-measurable and permanent. Just recall the example given above about planting a tree towards a selfless action. It is said in Gita verses 2/47, "do your karma but don't expect for the fruit of it". It does not mean that there is no fruit comes out of it. But the fruit will be un-limited and un-measurable and you cannot imagine or decide in what way it will come back to you in this birth, next birth or to your future generations.

But from the example of planting a tree for oxygen, we can clearly understand the vast benefit of doing selfless karmas. (3/10)

***

Oxygen (air) is so important for our breathing and survival and it comes from the tree. Tree and Oxygen – both are the most important things for humans. Without a human, the tree can survive, but without trees, a human cannot survive. So, the tree is most important for humans, because, fruit from the tree and oxygen from the tree both are needed for our living. Considering the importance and divinity embedded on the tree (oxygen, etc.), in ancient literature of India, we used to call them "Devata" – a divine thing.

What is or who is called Devata "The Divine"

A teacher and a student both are humans, but the teacher is more qualified than us in a particular subject, and his teachings will help us to develop and qualify to a higher level, we respectfully call him "teacher". The word "teacher" has more power than the word "student" does. The teacher is "up" and the student is "down". Since the teacher is more knowledgable, we seek knowledge from him and that's why the teacher is more 'divine' than us and we call him "Guru" – Guru is also a 'Devata = divine teacher".

It doesn't mean that trees and oxygen occupy the complete quality of the creator or the Supreme. Tree, oxygen, humans, animals all are creations under the Supreme. Per our need and necessity, we used to respect few creatures like the tree, oxygen, etc.

We all know that we cannot imagine life without oxygen. Oxygen or Air is called "VAYU" in Sanskrit or Hindi. And considering the above-mentioned importance of it, we used to respectfully mention it as "VAYU DEVATA", the "Divine Air".

So, if we need Oxygen, Fruits, Vitamins, etc., we need to respect trees and plant more and more trees (through selfless action and sacrifice). We can reciprocate carbon dioxide to trees. Plant more trees, generate more oxygen for us and future generations, exchange carbon dioxide.

Selfless action means - *planting a tree towards our obligatory duty to nature, and sacrifice means the time and money we use to cultivate it, and also sacrificing the feeling that "I did".*

In Bhagavad Gita, the word "Yagya" is used to represent such many sacrifices.

"Devata" – so many things like a tree, oxygen, water, food, fruits, etc. in nature and around us which has some divinity within it and very essential for human living. We need to cultivate and maintain such essential things in nature for our use, requirement, and protection.

That's why there are various methods like chanting mantras to invoke and gratifying a "Devata" for its help for our existence. We must respect, remember and must have gratitude each minute for whatever we are taking from anything or anybody for our existence.

We should always respect, remember, and must have gratitude towards grains, rains, farmers, vegetable sellers, etc. who continuously contribute to our well being and existence. Then only these contributions of nature will always sustain for you.

Suppose: If there is a person who has helped you with his car in a hospital emergency at night. After the emergency is over, you have returned the car to him without a word of gratitude. Later when somebody else has approached you for help with your car, you have refused it.

When the other man helped you with his car in an emergency, he was doing a selfless action being a "Devata" because you were seeking his help and it has been provided to you by him.

When you got a chance to reciprocate it for others, you refused it and lost the chance to become a "Devata" for the person who sought help from you.

When we don't remember or show gratitude for the help we got and when we refuse to reciprocate when others sought help from us, we are generating a lot of bad karma which ultimately makes our life miserable in a later stage.

Instead of maintaining a "Devata – divine attitude" in person and missing such chances of becoming a "Devata", we go to temples for the blessings of God. (but God knew about it).

Practice gratitude when somebody helps us.

Practice attitude to help when somebody seeks it from us.

Depending on the nature of gratitude and attitude, we can maintain many "Devatas, persons who possess a divine attitude" and we will be receiving help whenever or wherever we are in trouble.

Quote to note :

If you helped a child (not from your family), your son will get help when in need, wherever he is. The help your son got towards reciprocation of your help, may not be the same. It may be different. You have helped a child with food, your son got the help with a book which he was searching for a long time. Whatever you do selflessly for others, either way, it will come back.

(More in detail about the power of gratitude is mentioned in the book "The Magic" by Rhonda Byrne)

***

Quote to note :

If we are taking so many benefits from nature and not doing anything back to cultivate and maintain it for others, we are

Suppose, there are two farmers, with two different pieces of rice fields and the first farmer cultivated rice in his field and the second farmer did nothing. When the grains are ready, the second farmer has stolen grains from the first farmer's land at night.

***

The highly developed, self-realized, self-satisfied souls are those who regularly do a lot of self-less karmas for the benefit of others and happy with whatever earning has come. Like the 2nd shopkeeper in the above story who runs a shop for his livelihood but his intention, action, etc. by the mind are selfless.

One of the good examples of sacrifice is our mother at home. She prepares tasty food sincerely for the whole family; she never shows any weakness or tiredness to prepare the food, rather she will be happier and satisfied internally while doing the act.

After the preparation of food, does she take it first? Do you think any mother will say that she has prepared the tasty food by hard-work, so she wants to take it first and then will serve the leftover to other family members? NEVER.

She will even forget her hunger and will happily serve the whole family, she will never even worry if no food left for her. She will be happy even if we consume whole food.

The mother and the family members all have consumed the food. Even though she has prepared it, she got only our leftover.

But her internal satisfaction is so high because she did the action of making food without any kind of expectation in return from you. We are not even bothered to say thank you or the feeling of gratitude for the food we consumed.

Exactly, she has done a selfless action towards her obligatory duty thinking about the happiness and wellbeing of others.

Actually, here there is no importance to the action (karma) of making food because the real action is "selfless intention" in her mind.

When we enjoy a lot of benefits from nature and not contributing anything in return towards our duty, it's like stealing (collecting bad karmas) and somewhere in the future life or next birth, we need to repay. Many un-necessary life problems, hurdles, hindrances, health issues are happening because of that. (3/11-13).

Let's understand the importance of Selfless action &Sacrifice

Every creation starts and sprouts from a seed,

The seed needs water to sprout,

For water, rain is required,

For rain, water evaporation from the ocean is required,

For Ocean to evaporate, solar energy is required

From the above, we can learn and understand two things :

(1) Selfless Karma (action) and,

(2) Sacrifice.

Both action and sacrifice are required for the existence of nature and its creatures.

Seeds to do the **action** to sprout – **water** has to sacrifice for it.

Water to do the **action** – **rain** has to **sacrifice.**

For the **rain** to do the **action** – the ocean has to **sacrifice** by evaporating water.

For the **ocean** to do the evaporation **action** – Sun has to **sacrifice** its energy.

Like....

For a human to do the breathing **action, oxygen** is needed. **Trees** have to **sacrifice** their **oxygen** for humans.

Human to **sacrifice carbon dioxide** for **trees** to **act** upon...the chain goes on like this.

One to act, somebody's sacrifice is a must. And all the above actions and sacrifices are selfless.

Seeds expect nothing in return for its action & sacrifice.

Water expects nothing in return for its action & sacrifice.

Rain expects nothing in return for its action & sacrifice.

Ocean expects nothing in return for its action & sacrifice.

Sun expects nothing in return for its action & sacrifice.

In life...

Father works to feed children and wife selflessly.

Father through his salary feed his children and family – father won't expect anything from wife or children - Selfless action and sacrifice.

Mother prepares food and serves it to husband and children – Mother doesn't expect anything back.

But we children take the food and go. We may demand different tastes, we may point out the shortcomings in the food. No gratitude towards grains, cooked food, farmers or the creature (Supreme – Krishna) who has provided with everything. Those who possess such an attitude will suffer later sometime either in this life or next. (whatever bad karma we collect this way is called "curses" or "sins").

Quote to note :

We all have to perform some kind of selfless action and sacrifice for the benefit of others, then only the world and the existence of everything will sustain and continue.

All selfless karmas are like a boon for you (goodness in life)

All selfish (non-gratitude) karmas are curses and sins. (miserable life)

Ignorant people are unable to realize and understand the importance of **"selfless action and sacrifice,"** for the well-being of each other on the globe. They just enjoying their life lavishly and selfishly and unaware of the actual obligatory duties and actions, which must be performed being a human. Their thought and action are limited to physical enjoyment, attachment with close relations and accumulation of material wealth, etc. Their happiness and satisfaction are connected with those material things. They will always be worried to earn more, secure it and will be eager to enjoy every worldly pleasure.

But for selfless people, their peace and satisfaction are connected with their inner self and their main motto is to further spiritually develop towards the pathway to union with the Supreme Spirit. Since, such people are not interested to possess, attach or attract any physical and material things; they are not worried about any kind of loss and are self-centered and happy within them.

The self-confidence of such people is so high because every thought of them is connected directly with the Supreme.

So we all must follow, selfless action with sacrifice not just for our own family and relations, but for the well-being of the universe as a whole.

Once again, we can inspire from the role models life like Dr. APJ Abdul Kalam, Swami Vivekanand, Vinoba Bhave, etc.

There are so many people around the world who are still following the teachings of Dr. APJ Abdul Kalam, Vivekananda, Vinoba Bhave, etc. and to implement the life.

Every particle in the universe is doing some kind of selfless action, (even it is an atom) for the well-being and existence of the universe. (3/21).

Suppose, the Sun, rises every day, and spreads its light all over the world, and distributes its energy to every creature on the earth. Even the moon shines with its light. But what would happen, if one day, the Sun decided not to raise and not to perform its duty? The whole equilibrium of the world will disturb. Action and duties of everyone & everything will also disturb. The world will come to an end if the Sun stops from his duties. (3/22-24).

The self-realized, spiritually highly developed great scholars are also like the Sun that's why they are called illuminated people, those who have achieved universal wisdom.

The Sun lights the world and it distributes and spreads its energy to everyone. Same like Sun, spiritually highly developed great scholars will spread the light of wisdom to people selflessly who are striving to find solutions to come up from their selfish nature by ignorance. The great scholars must teach them how to achieve self-realization, material detachment and controlling mind and senses from desires. (3/25).

It won't be very easy to explain and teach about the selfless action, how it is to be performed, spiritual development, union with Supreme, etc. to a person who is enjoying worldly pleasures with material attachment. But slowly and gradually one can bring them up if they show little interest to develop from the present state. Forcefully cannot be done. (3/26).

The way and understanding of doing karma (action) will be different for different people. It depends on the dominance of any one of the Gunas (quality) out of three different Gunas (qualities). *Chapter-14 is about 3 Gunas (qualities), Sattva, Rajas & Tamas.*

Satvik Guna – Pure, selfless, luminous, free from material attachment, free from sorrow.

Rajasik Guna – Passion, pride, selfish desire and attachment, ego.

Tamasik Guna – Ignorant, over pride, lazy, slow, sleepy.

An over pride person by ignorance thinks that everything happens to him and his family is because of his involvement, power, and action.

So, for a spiritually developed person, it is important to balance the stability of mind when he sees an ignorant selfish person's action and attitude. His attitude is because of Rajasik or Tamasik guna dominance within him. They will be carrying a false belief in their mind that they are the owners and masters of whatever happens around them. (3/27).

If once we understood that the attitude and actions of every person are based on what guna (one out of three) dominating in them, we do not get angry with people, do not reject, discriminate or we will not get pained by their actions.

For eg: there is a newly married couple who starts their life together.

In the next few days, both of them understand each other's likes and dislikes.

The wife is a vegetarian, she likes milk and prefers a simple lifestyle *(Satwika guna is dominating within her, that reflects in her actions of lifestyle)*.

but her husband likes alcohol, non-vegetarian food and enjoys all worldly pleasures spending a lot of time with his friends, etc. (*Tamas Guna dominated within him, that reflects in his actions of lifestyle*).

Since they are husband and wife, they are forced to live together.

After a few months or so, the wife will start disliking his attitude and habits. Mental conflicts will start. Initially, she will request him to change the habits. But due to Tamas Guna dominance within him, he is forced to continue with his habits. He won't accept her plea. Whenever he comes home late in the evening, she will fight with him. Her mental pain will increase because she is forced to live with a person whose interests are opposite to her. There is no mental peace between them and harmony in the family.

Both of them possess the same attitude, habit, interests, and desires before they marry. Even after marriage, they follow their attitude and interest as before. Nobody has changed. But after the marriage, in a few days of togetherness and understanding of each other, they came to know that their attitude and habits are not similar. That non-similarity in both of their action and attitudes created the conflicts in between.

The wife is disliking his attitude and habits and is forcing him to change and follow her lifestyle and the husband is disliking her attitude and habits and is forcing her to follow his lifestyle.

Both of them are ignorant about the Guna dominance within them that's why there are mental conflicts, rejections, etc. will start and they will be forced to live an un-peaceful life by condemning each other by their shortcomings. The wife will say, I am perfect and the husband will say, I am perfect.

Actually, both are perfect but ignorant. Here the villain is "Guna" dominance within them that reflects in their attitudes. One possesses "Satwik" & one possesses "Rajasik or Tamasik". But both of them are unaware of the wisdom and understanding of "Guna" dominance.

If the wife understands that he is under the influence of "Rajasik & Tamasik" Guna, that reflects in his attitude and if the husband understands that she is under the influence of "Satwik" Guna that reflects in her attitude, then no conflicts will arise.

Since both of them are unaware of the influence of Guna, they both will fight each other, abuse each other, condemn each other and both of them will always try to change the attitude of one another. He wants to win her, she wants to win. They will forget their duties and responsibilities in life.

A Quote to note :

In the above story, there is confusion. Let me clear it.

Husband's attitude (non-vegetarian - lavish)

– Rajasik & Tamasik Guna.

Wife's attitude (vegetarian and simple)

– Satwik Guna.

But both are fighting. He wants to change her attitude to match him and she wants to change his attitude to match her.

If she or he is not intervening in their own chosen lifestyle by accepting, adjusting, managing, then both are maintaining the relationship to maintain harmony between them - based on "Satwik Guna".

*But at the same time as in the above story - **<u>wife's lifestyle is "Satwik", but her attitude towards him is "Rajasik and Tamasik,"</u>** that's why she is fighting and wants him to convert his lifestyle to match her. (she is satwik in lifestyle, but Rajasik & Tamasik in attitude towards her husband)*

She is forcing, pressurizing, torturing and is adamant in her decision that he must become vegetarian like her.

So, the concrete desire of her will be converted to anger & revenge and she will fight to win him, blame him, condemn him, etc. That's why, even being in a married relationship, both of them are mentally maintaining a gap and no harmony and mental peace there in between.

As long as she understands that he is a non-vegetarian because of the Rajasik and Tamasik guna dominancy within him, the situation will remain.

He will change only when the guna dominancy 'Rajasik and Tamasik' changes to Satwik through wisdom and intelligence.

***

This "Guna" issue and the example above, are not limited to between a husband and wife relation. We meet many people in life, some are close family members like mother, father, son, daughter, sister, brother, wife, husband, daughter-in-law, son-in-law, mother-in-law, father-in-law, uncles, aunties and the list of relationships goes on. Apart from that we meet many people outside of the family and develops a friendship with them throughout life.

Habits, attitudes, likes, dislikes, etc. of every person are different subject to Guna's dominance within them.

So, finally, the intelligent people who understood and aware of the Guna dominancy that reflects in one's action will never worry about the habits and attitudes of others. No conflicts or mental disturbances will arise. One will forgive others and will try to adjust to it if two people are forced to live together.

Suppose, a new baby is born, when he grew up, the mother understands that his attitude, habits, likes, dislikes are different from others. What she will do? Does she leave him, punish him, stop serving him, stop helping him? No. She will adjust, she will forgive and she will concentrate on her duty to serve his child better an better.

Quote to note :

If you are a mother, do your duty 100%. If your child's action un-satisfying you, try to adjust and forget it, a mother cannot curse him. Until you are alive and they are under your dependence, try to do your best for him/her.

If you are married, do your duty 100% irrespective of your spouse's actions. One's love and attention may be less than expected. This expectation will create problems and will disturb the mind. Make sure that whether you are 100% or not with your spouse. If you are unhappy and keeping a distance from your spouse because the actions of your partner are not matching with your expectations, it means you are also skipping from your duties and actions. You are fighting to win your spouse i.e. called physical and material desire. But if you are fighting to win your mind keeping it free of pain from other's actions, you get ultimate mental satisfaction and achieve spiritual development. We are not living here to win one and another on the earth, rather satisfy the Supreme by doing duties given by him.

Just imagine, that Krishna is watching you from the top :

(1) You are punishing one person badly in anger.

OR

(2) You are forgiving him, understanding the Guna dominance leaving the issue to God. You are cool, calm and

***

So, whenever we find a person with some attitude, habits, and actions opposite to yours, try to balance your mind, adjust with him understanding the Guna dominancy in each other. Otherwise, it will be difficult to live.

Nobody's attitude, habits, and actions will be the same. One will say my actions are right, others will say my actions are right. It is not our duty to check and verify whose actions are good or not. We are one out of billions of humans on the earth, we will meet many people and with some, we will maintain a temporary relationship. We must follow our attitude, habits, likes dislikes, etc. not try to change others. Let them follow theirs and you follow yours. We are liable to follow our own duties and actions, not liable to change others. Important is peace of mind, if it is disturbed, life will collapse.

If you are a doctor, follow your duty as a doctor, if you are an advocate; follow your duty as an advocate. The doctor cannot pressurize an advocate to do the actions of a doctor and an advocate cannot pressurize a doctor to perform advocacy. (3/29).

***

Then how to adjust the mind when it disturbs because of the miss-matching of each other's attitude, habits, and actions?

By dedicating and surrendering to the Supreme.

All that what disturbs you because of other's actions, submit to God. Don't develop too much expectation that the other person will change their action according to your taste. Forget the selfish thoughts like "I am" good and whatever "I" does is good. Don't think that you have the authority to decide who is good and who is wrong. Submit all actions to the Supreme and keep your mind cool, calm and quiet. Then only you will be able to develop a higher level of spirituality. The higher level of spirituality means, cultivating more "Satwik" guna within you. Once you achieve, how to balance the mind, You can easily manage every situation of your life, by fight-or-flight without disturbing anybody and without disturbing your mind.

Fighting in life does not mean that you have to fight and win a person, rather, it means that you have to win the mind by controlling your desires, attachments, un-wanted thoughts, tensions, sorrows, etc. which causes you to disturb your mind. A peaceful clear mind takes you soon to union with the Supreme.

Those who follow what is mentioned above, sincerely, satisfactorily, selflessly will be detached from any kind of material desire, physical bondage, and attachments.

Those who condemn it, reject it, un-follow it by ignorance
will be ruining their life.

We can see many people around us with disturbed and
un-satisfied minds because of not fulfilling their desires
and expectations in the way they want. They always carry
a doubtful and un-peaceful mind. Their happiness
depends on their winning of material desires and
attachments. (3/30-32).

Nobody can disobey the rule of nature. Even the great
scholars have to follow the rule of nature and to perform
actions subject to the guna dominance within them.

Senses are making attachments by the influence with
their respective field of interest and desires as some
people prefer sweet products and some people prefer
salty products, some people prefer to do good for the
society and some people prefer to do wrong for the
society. (3/30-34)

***

Influence to adopt other's action

(do the work of your interest, then only will excel)

As mentioned earlier, we are embedded with some
qualities by birth and some we develop and learn as we
are growing up. A singer by birth, that we can say, but we
cannot say an advocate by birth or doctor by birth. Each
one of us has immense talents within us, but some of the

dominant talents reflect in our life. If one person has three talents like writing, singing, drawing but the most dominant may be singing. Even though he has other talents, he is more interested to follow the singing.

But if you want to become a doctor, engineer, advocate, entrepreneur or so, you need a professional qualification in the respective field. Apart from that, your interest in choosing the subject is there. One person has a keen interest in the subject biology and he has chosen the same subject as his main till +2. Not even 10% interest in maths. So, he decided to become a Doctor. But his parents forced him to become an engineer or advocate, then conflicts and confusion will arise in his mind.

The influence of other's actions means, being a good talented singer your duties and actions will be to become a good singer. But one of your friends is a writer and he has a lot of name, fame, and money than you. This will disturb your mind because of the influence of the success of your friend who is a writer.

The same may happen in the other professions and professionals too. An engineer may un-happy seeing his friend's high success, who is a doctor.

A singer can think to skip their profession from Singer to writer and engineers can think to skip his profession from Engineer to Doctor. In today's world, a singer can try to become a writer, but an engineer can't try to become a doctor unless he is academically qualified.

But the success of others can influence us to skip from our talents and to adopt others. But it is not necessary that we also get success in that profession if we adopt it.

Whether you get high success or not, you will always feel comfortable and satisfactory working with your own talents only. Adopting others by influence will never make you successful.

This is the same as we intervene in other's duties and actions as mentioned above.

Concentrate your interests, own duties, and talents which will only give you success and permanent satisfaction. Even if the success is less, you can show your perfection in your field of own interest.

The desire to skipping from your talent of interest to other's talent of interest also develops by the "Rajas & Tamas" guna dominance within you. Whenever the "Rajas & Tamas" guna dominates in your action, the mind works as an enemy for you.

When "Rajas & Tamas" guna dominate in your actions, your excellent qualities, talents, selfless attitude, wisdom, intelligence, detachment, etc. will be hidden like a clear mirror is covered by smoke.

When we are jealous and angry with others, we will see only bad in others because we lose the ability to see good in others. (3/38).

***

Quote to note :

When our mind is disturbed, we are the patient. But we blame others and trying to treat others.

***

The level of our intelligence depends on what guna dominance in every thought and action.

***

The senses are great, but the mind is greater than the senses because senses are connected with the mind and master of it. But intelligence and wisdom are great than mind because through intelligence and wisdom we can clean the dirt in our mind to satisfy our Soul, which is greater than everything.

When we achieve the wisdom and understanding of the Soul, our desires, attachment, etc. will come down, Satvik guna will increase and we will find permanent peace in mind.

Chapter-3 Slokhas in English Text for Quick Reference

1,2

arjuna uvācha
jyāyasī chet karmaṇas te matā buddhir janārdana
tat kim karmaṇi ghore mām niyojayasi keśhava
vyāmiśhreṇeva vākyena buddhim mohayasīva me
tad ekam vada niśhchitya yena śhreyo 'ham āpnuyām

3

śhrī bhagavān uvācha
loke 'smin dvi-vidhā niṣhṭhā purā proktā mayānagha
jñāna-yogena sāṅkhyānām karma-yogena yoginām

4

na karmaṇām anārambhān naiṣhkarmyam puruṣho 'śhnute
na cha sannyasanād eva siddhim samadhigachchhati

5

na hi kaśhchit kṣhaṇam api jātu tiṣhṭhatyakarma-kṛit
kāryate hyavaśhaḥ karma sarvaḥ prakṛiti-jair guṇaiḥ

6

karmendriyāṇi sanyamya ya āste manasā smaran
indriyārthān vimūḍhātmā mithyāchāraḥ sa uchyate

7

yas tvindriyāṇi manasā niyamyārabhate 'rjuna
karmendriyaiḥ karma-yogam asaktaḥ sa viśiṣhyate

8

niyataṁ kuru karma tvaṁ karma jyāyo hyakarmaṇaḥ
śharīra-yātrāpi cha te na prasiddhyed akarmaṇaḥ

9

yajñārthāt karmaṇo 'nyatra loko 'yaṁ karma-bandhanaḥ
tad-arthaṁ karma kaunteya mukta-saṅgaḥ samāchara

10

saha-yajñāḥ prajāḥ sṛiṣhṭvā purovācha prajāpatiḥ
anena prasaviṣhyadhvam eṣha vo 'stviṣhṭa-kāma-dhuk

11

devān bhāvayatānena te devā bhāvayantu vaḥ
parasparaṁ bhāvayantaḥ śhreyaḥ param avāpsyatha

12

iṣhṭān bhogān hi vo devā dāsyante yajña-bhāvitāḥ
tair dattān apradāyaibhyo yo bhuṅkte stena eva saḥ

13

yajña-śhiṣhṭāśhinaḥ santo muchyante sarva-kilbiṣhaiḥ
bhuñjate te tvaghaṁ pāpā ye pachantyātma-kāraṇāt

14

annād bhavanti bhūtāni parjanyād anna-sambhavaḥ
yajñād bhavati parjanyo yajñaḥ karma-samudbhavaḥ

15

karma brahmodbhavaṁ viddhi brahmākṣhara-samudbhavam
tasmāt sarva-gataṁ brahma nityaṁ yajñe pratiṣhṭhitam

16

evaṁ pravartitaṁ chakraṁ nānuvartayatīha yaḥ
aghāyur indriyārāmo moghaṁ pārtha sa jīvati

17

yas tvātma-ratir eva syād ātma-tṛiptaśh cha mānavaḥ
ātmanyeva cha santuṣhṭas tasya kāryaṁ na vidyate

18

naiva tasya kṛitenārtho nākṛiteneha kaśhchana
na chāsya sarva-bhūteṣhu kaśhchid artha-vyapāśhrayaḥ

19

tasmād asaktaḥ satataṁ kāryaṁ karma samāchara
asakto hyācharan karma param āpnoti pūruṣhaḥ

20, 21

karmaṇaiva hi sansiddhim āsthitā janakādayaḥ
loka-saṅgraham evāpi sampaśhyan kartum arhasi
yad yad ācharati śhreṣhṭhas tat tad evetaro janaḥ
sa yat pramāṇaṁ kurute lokas tad anuvartate

22

na me pārthāsti kartavyaṁ triṣhu lokeṣhu kiñchana
nānavāptam avāptavyaṁ varta eva cha karmaṇi

23

yadi hyahaṁ na varteyaṁ jātu karmaṇyatandritaḥ
mama vartmānuvartante manuṣhyāḥ pārtha sarvaśhaḥ

24

utsīdeyur ime lokā na kuryāṁ karma ched aham
sankarasya cha kartā syām upahanyām imāḥ prajāḥ

25

saktāḥ karmaṇyavidvānso yathā kurvanti bhārata
kuryād vidvāns tathāsaktaśh chikīrṣhur loka-saṅgraham

26

na buddhi-bhedaṁ janayed ajñānāṁ karma-saṅginām
joṣhayet sarva-karmāṇi vidvān yuktaḥ samācharan

27

prakṛiteḥ kriyamāṇāni guṇaiḥ karmāṇi sarvaśhaḥ
ahankāra-vimūḍhātmā kartāham iti manyate

28

tattva-vit tu mahā-bāho guṇa-karma-vibhāgayoḥ
guṇā guṇeṣhu vartanta iti matvā na sajjate

29

prakṛiter guṇa-sammūḍhāḥ sajjante guṇa-karmasu
tān akṛitsna-vido mandān kṛitsna-vin na vichālayet

30

mayi sarvāṇi karmāṇi sannyasyādhyātma-chetasā
nirāśhīr nirmamo bhūtvā yudhyasva vigata-jvaraḥ

31

ye me matam idaṁ nityam anutiṣhṭhanti mānavāḥ
śhraddhāvanto 'nasūyanto muchyante te 'pi karmabhiḥ

32

ye tvetad abhyasūyanto nānutiṣhṭhanti me matam
sarva-jñāna-vimūḍhāns tān viddhi naṣhṭān achetasaḥ

33

sadṛiśham cheṣhṭate svasyāḥ prakṛiter jñānavān api
prakṛitiṁ yānti bhūtāni nigrahaḥ kiṁ kariṣhyati

34

indriyasyendriyasyārthe rāga-dveṣhau vyavasthitau
tayor na vaśham āgachchhet tau hyasya paripanthinau

35

śhreyān swa-dharmo viguṇaḥ para-dharmāt sv-anuṣhṭhitāt
swa-dharme nidhanaṁ śhreyaḥ para-dharmo bhayāvahaḥ

36

arjuna uvācha
atha kena prayukto 'yaṁ pāpaṁ charati pūruṣhaḥ
anichchhann api vārṣhṇeya balād iva niyojitaḥ

37

śhrī bhagavān uvācha
kāma eṣha krodha eṣha rajo-guṇa-samudbhavaḥ
mahāśhano mahā-pāpmā viddhyenam iha vairiṇam

38

dhūmenāvriyate vahnir yathādarśho malena cha
yatholbenāvṛito garbhas tathā tenedam āvṛitam

39

āvṛitaṁ jñānam etena jñānino nitya-vairiṇā
kāma-rūpeṇa kaunteya duṣhpūreṇānalena cha

40

indriyāṇi mano buddhir asyādhiṣhṭhānam uchyate
etair vimohayatyeṣha jñānam āvṛitya dehinam

41

tasmāt tvam indriyāṇyādau niyamya bharatarṣhabha
pāpmānaṁ prajahi hyenaṁ jñāna-vijñāna-nāśhanam

42

indriyāṇi parāṇyāhur indriyebhyaḥ param manaḥ
manasas tu parā buddhir yo buddheḥ paratas tu saḥ

43

evaṁ buddheḥ paraṁ buddhvā sanstabhyātmānam ātmanā
jahi śhatruṁ mahā-bāho kāma-rūpaṁ durāsadam

Contact

9839093003

myrichindia@gmail.com

facebook.com/drjagadeeshpillai

youtube.com/drjagadeeshpillai